L.S. IGNACIUS

Reality Distortion Field

A Blueprint for Visionary Leadership and Achievement

First published by Deep Thoughts Books 2024

Copyright © 2024 by L.S. Ignacius

All rights reserved. No part of this publication may be reproduced, stored or transmitted in any form or by any means, electronic, mechanical, photocopying, recording, scanning, or otherwise without written permission from the publisher. It is illegal to copy this book, post it to a website, or distribute it by any other means without permission.

L.S. Ignacius asserts the moral right to be identified as the author of this work.

L.S. Ignacius has no responsibility for the persistence or accuracy of URLs for external or third-party Internet Websites referred to in this publication and does not guarantee that any content on such Websites is, or will remain, accurate or appropriate.

Designations used by companies to distinguish their products are often claimed as trademarks. All brand names and product names used in this book and on its cover are trade names, service marks, trademarks and registered trademarks of their respective owners. The publishers and the book are not associated with any product or vendor mentioned in this book. None of the companies referenced within the book have endorsed the book.

First edition

This book was professionally typeset on Reedsy.
Find out more at reedsy.com

Contents

1. Introduction — 1
2. The Philosophy of the Reality Distortion Field — 9
3. Implementing RDF in Your Life – The Step-by-Step Guide — 16
4. Overcoming Challenges — 23
5. Scaling the Reality Distortion Field — 29
6. The Legacy of Shaping Reality — 35
7. Appendix — 39

1

Introduction

Welcome to the Power of Perception

What if I told you that the limits of what you can achieve are not dictated by external circumstances, but by the boundaries of your perception? The **Reality Distortion Field (RDF)** is not just a concept—it's a powerful mindset that allows you to shape your world and inspire others to believe in your vision, even when it seems impossible.

Originally coined to describe the extraordinary influence of Steve Jobs, the RDF philosophy transcends the tech world. It is a way of thinking and acting that enables anyone to bend the constraints of conventional thought, challenge the status quo, and create breakthroughs in their personal and professional lives.

At its core, the Reality Distortion Field is about conviction, influence, and the art of perception. It's a tool to turn ambitious dreams into achievable realities, not by ignoring the truth but by redefining it. Think of it as the ability to see a future so vividly that others begin to see it too—and, more importantly, to act on it.

But RDF isn't magic, and it's not just for visionary leaders. It's a learnable skill, a practice that can empower you to challenge limitations, inspire others, and unlock your potential.

Why Perception Matters

Perception shapes reality. How you see yourself, the world, and your opportunities determines the actions you take and the outcomes you achieve. The power of perception isn't just about seeing things differently—it's about reshaping what's possible.

For instance:

- A runner who visualizes crossing the finish line before a race often performs better than one who fixates on the obstacles ahead.
- A leader who radiates unwavering belief in their vision can rally teams to overcome challenges, even in the face of uncertainty.
- An individual who embraces the mindset of "why

not me?" can turn audacious goals into achievable milestones.

The key takeaway? When you master the power of perception, you unlock the ability to rewrite the narrative of your life.

The Invitation

This book invites you to step into the world of the Reality Distortion Field. Whether you're seeking personal growth, professional success, or deeper connections, the RDF philosophy can help you see what others cannot and achieve what others dare not.

By the end of this journey, you'll not only understand how RDF works but also how to apply its principles in your own life. You'll learn how to:

- Craft a vision so compelling it becomes contagious.
- Build unshakable self-belief and emotional intelligence.
- Cultivate influence through communication and empathy.
- Balance ambition with ethical grounding.

Are you ready to step beyond your limits? Welcome to the power of perception—and the beginning of your transformation.

What is the Reality Distortion Field (RDF)?

The **Reality Distortion Field** (RDF) is the ability to reshape perceptions, defy conventional limits, and inspire belief in the impossible. At its essence, RDF allows you to project a vision so compelling and convincing that it not only transforms your perspective but also influences others to see the world through your lens.

Think of RDF as the intersection of unwavering self-belief, persuasive communication, and strategic action. It's not about ignoring reality—it's about re framing it to align with your aspirations. RDF empowers you to see possibilities where others see problems and to act boldly even when the odds are stacked against you.

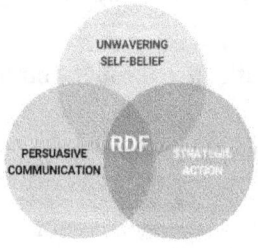

This mindset extends beyond charisma or confidence. It's a holistic approach that combines vision, influence, and execution to transform both personal and professional outcomes.

The Origin of the Term and Its Connection to Steve Jobs

The term **Reality Distortion Field** (RDF) was first coined by Apple engineer Bud Tribble in 1981, during the early days of the Macintosh project. Tribble used the phrase to describe Steve Jobs's extraordinary ability to bend perceptions and inspire belief in even the most implausible ideas. It was a nod to an episode of *Star Trek*, where aliens used a "reality distortion field" to influence those around them.

Jobs's *Reality Distortion Field* was a blend of intense charisma, unwavering confidence, and a refusal to accept conventional limitations. According to Tribble, it wasn't just about persuasion—it was about creating an alternate reality where the impossible seemed achievable. This unique ability often pushed Apple's teams beyond what they thought was possible, driving them to innovate and deliver groundbreaking products like the Macintosh, iPhone, and iPad.

Jobs's RDF could be polarizing. While some saw it as manipulation, others admired it as a visionary leadership tool. Tribble and other team members observed how Jobs could rally people around a vision with sheer passion, often convincing them to overcome immense technical hurdles or meet impossible deadlines. His belief in the field's power was so strong that he made his teams believe in themselves, achieving results that shaped the tech industry forever.

For example:

- When Jobs envisioned the first Macintosh, he insisted it be "insanely great," pushing his team to innovate beyond the limitations of existing technology.
- He convinced skeptical investors and partners to back his vision, often without fully formed prototypes to show for it.

The term has since become synonymous with Jobs's legacy, but it also serves as a broader metaphor for leadership, innovation, and the ability to challenge the status quo. It's not just about persuasion—it's about rewriting the rules of what can be achieved.

Why Mastering RDF Can Transform Your Personal and Professional Life

RDF isn't reserved for tech moguls or industry pioneers. Its principles can be applied to elevate your life in remarkable ways, whether you're striving for career success, personal growth, or stronger relationships.

Personal Transformation

- **Break Free from Self-Limiting Beliefs:** RDF helps you recognize that many barriers are self-imposed. By re framing your mindset, you open doors to new possibilities.
- **Achieve Lofty Goals:** By crafting a clear vision and believing in its achievability, you unlock the courage and focus to pursue what once seemed unattainable.
- **Enhance Resilience:** RDF cultivates the mental strength to face challenges with optimism and creativity, turning setbacks into stepping stones.

Professional Impact

- **Inspire and Lead:** Whether you're managing a team or running your own business, RDF empowers you to create a shared vision that motivates

and energizes others.
- **Innovate Beyond Constraints:** RDF trains you to think outside the box, enabling groundbreaking ideas and solutions that disrupt the status quo.
- **Build Influence:** By mastering persuasive communication and emotional intelligence, you can rally support, win partnerships, and grow your network.

Why It Matters Now

In today's rapidly changing world, the ability to adapt and influence is more critical than ever. Markets evolve, industries shift, and challenges grow more complex. Those who master the art of reshaping reality rise above these challenges, leveraging them as opportunities for growth and innovation.

The Reality Distortion Field is more than a philosophy—it's a superpower you can cultivate. By embracing its principles, you take control of your narrative, inspire those around you, and unlock the full potential of your life.

In the chapters ahead, we'll break down exactly how you can implement RDF in your everyday life, starting with the core belief that reality is not fixed—it's yours to design.

2

The Philosophy of the Reality Distortion Field

> **Philosophy:** the study of the fundamental nature of knowledge, reality, and existence, especially when considered as an academic discipline.

The Reality Distortion Field (RDF) isn't just a tool—it's a way of thinking, a philosophy that challenges the very fabric of how we understand reality. It is about rewriting the narrative of what's possible, not only in the external world but also within ourselves.

This chapter explores the deeper principles that underpin RDF, showing how it operates on the interplay of belief, perception, and influence. By the end, you'll see RDF not as a mystical force but as a practical mindset that can be cultivated by anyone willing to challenge limits and embrace a visionary approach to life.

1. RDF as a Philosophy, Not Just a Skill

At first glance, the Reality Distortion Field may seem like a clever trick—a way to convince others to believe in something extraordinary. However, RDF is much more profound. It's a philosophy rooted in the belief that perception defines reality.

Think about this: the world you experience is shaped by how you interpret it. This isn't just about optimism versus pessimism—it's about the lens through which you perceive challenges, opportunities, and even your own potential.

RDF and Self-Belief

At its heart, RDF begins with the individual. If you can't convince yourself of the plausibility of your vision, you'll never inspire others to believe it. RDF demands a profound level of self-belief that transcends doubts and external limitations. This is not arrogance; it's conviction.

Vision vs. Manipulation

One of the philosophical tensions within RDF is its dual nature:

- **Visionary Application:** Inspiring others to see beyond their limits and collaborate on something extraordinary.
- **Manipulative Potential:** Using influence to distort facts for personal gain.

The ethical boundary between these two paths defines whether RDF uplifts or deceives. True RDF practitioners align their influence with authenticity and purpose, ensuring their vision serves both themselves and others.

2. The Science Behind the Magic

While RDF feels like a superpower, its roots are grounded in psychological and neurological principles. Understanding these can demystify the concept and make it more accessible.

The Neuroscience of Belief

- **Neuroplasticity:** The brain's ability to rewire itself based on thought patterns. When you repeatedly visualize success or challenge limiting beliefs, you literally reshape your brain's structure to align with that reality.
- **Mirror Neurons:** These neurons fire when we observe someone else's actions or emotions, allowing leaders with strong RDF to inspire and influence others by embodying confidence and determination.

Cognitive Biases at Play

RDF leverages natural biases, such as:

- **Confirmation Bias:** People tend to seek evidence that supports their existing beliefs. By projecting conviction, you can create an environment where others subconsciously align with your vision.
- **Optimism Bias:** A tendency to overestimate positive outcomes, which, when harnessed effectively, fuels the momentum needed to overcome challenges.

Emotional Resonance

RDF is most effective when it connects emotionally. When people feel inspired, hopeful, or intrigued, they're more likely to support your vision. This is why great leaders focus on storytelling, empathy, and emotional intelligence as part of their RDF arsenal.

3. Iconic Examples of RDF in Action

To truly understand RDF, it helps to see it in action. Let's examine a few individuals who exemplified this philosophy:

Steve Jobs: Redefining Innovation

Steve Jobs didn't just sell products—he sold a vision of a better future. His RDF allowed Apple to innovate relentlessly, often pushing teams to achieve "impossible" deadlines and features. For example:

- When Jobs wanted the first iPhone to have a sleek glass screen, engineers told him it couldn't be done within the timeline. Jobs' unwavering belief—and insistence—motivated them to deliver the seemingly impossible.

Historical Leaders Who Bended Reality

- **Mahatma Gandhi:** Gandhi's vision of nonviolent resistance seemed naive in the face of British imperialism, yet his RDF inspired millions to believe in and achieve India's independence.
- **Walt Disney:** Disney imagined a world where animated films and theme parks could transport people to magical places. His ability to project that vision turned financial skepticism into global success.

Everyday Applications of RDF

- **Personal Development:** An individual who consistently visualizes their ideal career and takes steps toward it often discovers opportunities others overlook.
- **Relationships:** Convincing a partner, friend, or colleague to believe in a shared dream or resolve conflict often hinges on presenting a vision they can buy into.

The Reality Distortion Field isn't just about charisma or rhetoric; it's a mindset that starts with you. By cultivating an RDF, you're not just bending reality—you're crafting a better one.

In the next chapter, we'll explore how to take these

philosophical foundations and apply them step by step to reshape your world, influence others, and bring ambitious visions to life.

3

Implementing RDF in Your Life – The Step-by-Step Guide

The Reality Distortion Field (RDF) is not just a lofty concept; it's a practical framework that anyone can apply to their life. By following a structured process, you can begin to reshape your perception, influence others, and manifest ambitious visions into reality.

This chapter breaks down the key steps to cultivate and implement RDF in your daily life, offering actionable insights and tools to help you unlock its transformative power.

Step 1: Define a Clear and Compelling Vision

RDF begins with a vision—a vivid, detailed image of the outcome you want to achieve. Without clarity, it's impossible to inspire yourself or others.

Crafting Your Vision

1. **Be Specific:** What does success look like to you? Use tangible details to make your vision feel real.
2. **Tap Into Emotion:** Why does this vision matter to you? Connecting emotionally will fuel your commitment.

3. **Challenge Conventional Limits:** Don't just aim for what seems achievable—dream bigger. RDF thrives on audacity.

Exercise:

Write a vivid paragraph describing your ultimate goal. Include sensory details, emotions, and the impact it will have on your life and others.

Step 2: Build Unshakable Self-Belief

Before you can convince others to buy into your vision, you must believe in it with absolute certainty. RDF demands unwavering confidence that your vision is not only possible but inevitable.

Strategies to Strengthen Self-Belief

- **Positive Visualization:** Spend time each day visualizing your vision as if it's already a reality.
- **Reframe Doubts:** Turn limiting beliefs into empowering ones. Instead of "I can't," ask, "How can I?"
- **Celebrate Small Wins:** Each step forward reinforces your belief in achieving the larger goal.

Step 3: Communicate with Impact

The ability to convey your vision persuasively is a cornerstone of RDF. Your words, tone, and energy must inspire others to see what you see.

The Art of Persuasion

- **Storytelling:** Share narratives that emotionally connect with your audience and highlight the importance of your vision.
- **Clarity and Confidence:** Speak as though your vision is not a possibility but a certainty.
- **Empathy:** Understand your audience's needs and concerns, and tailor your message to address them.

Pro Tip: Use vivid metaphors and examples to make your vision relatable and memorable.

Step 4: Influence Through Action

Actions speak louder than words. People are more likely to believe in your vision if they see you taking consistent steps to make it a reality.

How to Align Actions with Vision

- **Lead by Example:** Demonstrate the commitment and energy you expect from others.
- **Take Bold Risks:** Show that you're willing to push beyond conventional limits to achieve your goals.
- **Consistency is Key:** Follow through on your promises to build trust and credibility.

Exercise:
Identify one actionable step you can take today to bring your vision closer to reality.

Step 5: Cultivate Emotional Intelligence

RDF isn't about brute force—it's about influence, and influence is rooted in emotional intelligence. Understanding and managing emotions—both yours and others'—is critical for success.

Emotional Intelligence in Practice

- **Self-Awareness:** Recognize your emotional triggers and manage them effectively.
- **Empathy:** Understand the perspectives of others and validate their feelings.
- **Adaptability:** Stay calm and resourceful in the

face of obstacles or resistance.

Step 6: Create a Contagious Energy

RDF thrives on momentum. When people feel energized and inspired by your vision, they'll naturally want to support it.

How to Generate Energy

- **Passion is Contagious:** Share your enthusiasm authentically—it's impossible to fake.
- **Celebrate Progress:** Acknowledge milestones, no matter how small, to keep spirits high.
- **Foster Collaboration:** Invite others to contribute their ideas and talents, creating a shared sense of ownership.

Step 7: Balance Ambition with Ethical Integrity

As powerful as RDF can be, it's essential to use it responsibly. True leadership is grounded in authenticity and a commitment to ethical principles.

Maintaining Integrity

- **Align Actions with Values:** Ensure your vision serves not just your interests but also those of others.
- **Be Transparent:** Communicate openly about challenges and setbacks to build trust.
- **Prioritize Long-Term Impact:** Focus on creating sustainable, meaningful change rather than short-term wins.

Implementing RDF in your life is not about becoming someone else—it's about unleashing the fullest, boldest version of yourself. By combining a clear vision, unshakable belief, persuasive communication, and ethical action, you can transform not only your reality but also the lives of those around you.

Whether you're leading a team, building a business, or pursuing personal growth. Let's explore how this philosophy can redefine what's possible in every corner of your life.

4

Overcoming Challenges

No great transformation comes without resistance. The path to mastering the *Reality Distortion Field* (RDF) will be filled with obstacles—both internal and external. These challenges aren't roadblocks but opportunities to refine your vision, strengthen your resolve, and evolve into a more resilient individual.

This chapter explores common challenges you may encounter while implementing RDF, offering actionable strategies to overcome them and turn setbacks into stepping stones.

1. Internal Challenges: Breaking Free from Self-Limiting Beliefs

One of the greatest hurdles is often within: the voice of doubt that tells you, "It's impossible," or, "You're not enough."

Common Internal Barriers

- **Fear of Failure:** The anxiety that mistakes will lead to judgment or ruin.
- **Imposter Syndrome:** Feeling unworthy or incapable despite evidence of your abilities.
- **Analysis Paralysis:** Overthinking every step, delaying action, and losing momentum.

How to Overcome Internal Challenges

- **Reframe Failure as Feedback:** Every mistake is a learning opportunity. Instead of fearing failure, ask, "What is this teaching me?"
- **Adopt a Growth Mindset:** Remind yourself that abilities aren't fixed; they evolve through effort and learning.
- **Use Daily Affirmations:** Replace negative self-talk with empowering statements that reinforce your belief in your vision.

Exercise:

Write down three self-limiting beliefs you hold and reframe them into empowering affirmations. For example:

- "I'm not ready for this challenge" becomes "I am prepared to grow and adapt to meet this challenge."

2. External Challenges: Facing Skepticism and Resistance

When you present a bold vision, you'll inevitably encounter doubters, critics, and naysayers. This resistance often comes from those who can't see beyond their own limitations.

Why Resistance Occurs

- **Fear of Change:** People are often uncomfortable with the unfamiliar.
- **Projection of Their Limits:** Critics project their insecurities onto you.
- **Lack of Context:** Others may not fully understand your vision or process.

How to Handle Skepticism

- **Respond, Don't React:** Stay calm and address concerns with clarity and confidence.
- **Lead with Results:** Demonstrate progress through tangible actions and achievements.
- **Filter Feedback:** Differentiate between constructive criticism (which helps you improve) and baseless negativity (which you can ignore).

Pro Tip: Use storytelling to make your vision relatable and address skepticism. When people understand the "why" behind your ideas, they're more likely to support them.

3. Practical Challenges: Navigating Resources and Logistics

Even with the most compelling vision, practical constraints like time, money, and access to resources can feel overwhelming.

Strategies for Overcoming Practical Challenges

- **Start Small:** Focus on achievable steps that build momentum toward your larger goal.
- **Leverage Networks:** Collaborate with others who can offer skills, resources, or support.

- **Be Resourceful:** Creativity often thrives under constraints. Ask yourself, "How can I achieve this with what I have?"

4. Emotional Challenges: Managing Stress and Burnout

Pushing boundaries requires energy and resilience, but the pursuit of big dreams can also be draining. Managing your emotional well-being is crucial to maintaining momentum.

Signs of Burnout

- Persistent exhaustion, even after rest.
- Loss of motivation or passion for your vision.
- Feeling disconnected from yourself or others.

How to Prevent and Recover from Burnout

- **Practice Self-Care:** Schedule time for rest, hobbies, and physical health.
- **Set Realistic Expectations:** Allow yourself room for setbacks and avoid perfectionism.
- **Reconnect with Your Why:** Reflect on the deeper purpose behind your vision to reignite your passion.

5. Balancing Reality with Aspiration

While RDF encourages bold thinking, there's a fine line between inspiring others and pushing too far into the realm of unrealistic expectations.

Avoiding Overstretching

- **Stay Grounded in Data:** Use facts and research to support your vision when necessary.
- **Adapt When Needed:** Flexibility isn't weakness—it's wisdom.
- **Build Trust Through Consistency:** Deliver small wins consistently to strengthen credibility.

Challenges are not signs to turn back; they are proof that you're forward. Every doubt, obstacle, or criticism is an opportunity to strengthen your RDF and refine your approach.

By mastering the art of overcoming both internal and external resistance, you not only bring your vision closer to reality but also grow into a stronger, more capable individual.

5

Scaling the Reality Distortion Field

Mastering the Reality Distortion Field (RDF) on a personal level is transformative, but its true power lies in scaling it. Scaling RDF means extending its influence to teams, organizations, and communities, amplifying your ability to inspire and achieve ambitious visions.

This chapter explores how to take RDF beyond yourself, creating an ecosystem where innovation thrives, collaboration deepens, and bold ideas take root and flourish.

1. Building a Shared Vision

When scaling RDF, it's no longer just your vision—it's a collective one. A shared vision aligns individuals around a common purpose, inspiring unity and collective effort.

How to Build a Shared Vision

- **Involve Stakeholders Early:** People are more likely to support what they help create. Invite input to make the vision inclusive.
- **Communicate the Big Picture:** Help others understand how their roles contribute to the overall success of the vision.
- **Appeal to Emotions:** Facts inform, but emotions move people. Share why this vision matters on a personal and societal level.

Example: Steve Jobs didn't just sell computers— he sold the idea of "changing the world" through technology, a purpose his team could rally behind.

2. Creating a Culture of Possibility

To scale RDF effectively, you need to cultivate an environment where ambition, creativity, and risk-taking are encouraged.

Principles of a Possibility-Driven Culture

- **Celebrate Bold Ideas:** Reward those who think big, even if their ideas don't always work out.
- **Encourage Experimentation:** Create safe spaces for people to try, fail, and learn without fear of

judgment.
- **Model Optimism:** As a leader, your belief in the vision sets the tone for the group. Radiate confidence, even during challenges.

Pro Tip: Use team rituals—such as brainstorming sessions or "failure celebrations"—to reinforce a culture of creativity and resilience.

3. Developing a Network of RDF Champions

Scaling RDF isn't about shouldering everything yourself—it's about empowering others to become advocates for the vision.

How to Empower Others

- **Identify Champions:** Look for individuals who are naturally influential and share your passion for the vision.
- **Train Them:** Provide tools and knowledge so they can effectively communicate and embody the RDF principles.
- **Delegate Ownership:** Give champions autonomy over aspects of the vision to deepen their commitment and amplify their impact.

Case Study: Elon Musk empowers his teams at Tesla

and SpaceX by instilling a shared belief that their work isn't just about building products—it's about solving humanity's biggest challenges.

4. Leveraging Technology to Amplify Your Reach

Technology is a powerful enabler for scaling RDF. It allows you to connect with larger audiences, share your message widely, and gather support at unprecedented levels.

Key Tools for Scaling RDF

- **Social Media:** Share stories, progress updates, and behind-the-scenes insights to engage and inspire your audience.
- **Collaborative Platforms:** Use tools like Slack, Trello, or Notion to keep your team aligned and focused.
- **Digital Campaigns:** Leverage email marketing, webinars, and online communities to rally support for your vision.

5. Overcoming Resistance at Scale

Scaling RDF inevitably attracts skeptics and resistance, particularly as your influence grows. Managing resistance effectively is crucial to maintaining momentum.

Tactics to Address Resistance

- **Anticipate Pushback:** Understand the concerns of your audience and address them proactively.
- **Show Tangible Results:** Highlight wins, milestones, or testimonials to demonstrate progress and credibility.
- **Remain Adaptable:** Be willing to adjust your approach to meet the needs of different groups without compromising your core vision.

Pro Tip: Frame resistance as a natural part of growth. Reassure your team that pushback is evidence of bold progress.

6. Measuring and Sustaining Momentum

To ensure long-term success, it's vital to track the impact of your scaled RDF efforts and maintain the energy behind them.

How to Measure Success

- **Quantitative Metrics:** Monitor key performance indicators (KPIs) such as engagement rates, project completion times, or revenue growth.

- **Qualitative Feedback:** Gather testimonials, surveys, and informal feedback to gauge emotional alignment with the vision.

Sustaining Momentum

- **Recognize Contributions:** Regularly acknowledge and celebrate the efforts of those contributing to the vision.
- **Evolve the Vision:** As milestones are achieved, refine and expand your goals to keep the momentum alive.
- **Renew Energy:** Periodically revisit the "why" behind your vision to reignite passion among your team and followers.

Scaling the Reality Distortion Field transforms it from a personal tool into a collective movement. By fostering a shared vision, empowering champions, and leveraging technology, you can amplify its impact far beyond your immediate sphere of influence.

In the next chapter, we'll explore real-life case studies of individuals and organizations that successfully scaled RDF, analyzing the lessons we can learn from their journeys. These stories will inspire and guide you as you expand your own RDF to unprecedented levels.

6

The Legacy of Shaping Reality

As you've journeyed through this exploration of the Reality Distortion Field (RDF), one thing becomes crystal clear: the ability to reshape perception and redefine what's possible isn't reserved for a select few. It's a skill—a philosophy—that anyone can cultivate with intention, practice, and resilience.

This conclusion isn't an ending but a call to action. You now have the tools to harness the power of RDF, step into your potential, and leave a lasting impact on the world around you. Let's reflect on the legacy you can create by shaping reality.

The Ripple Effect of RDF

Every bold idea, innovative solution, or paradigm-shifting moment begins with someone who dares to see beyond limitations. By mastering RDF, you not only transform your own life but also inspire others to reimagine what they believe is possible.

Your Influence Goes Beyond You

- **Empowering Others:** Your confidence and vision can ignite potential in those around you.
- **Creating Movements:** The ripple effect of your RDF can unite people behind a shared purpose.
- **Redefining Standards:** By challenging the status quo, you set new benchmarks for what can be achieved.

Remember: The reality you shape today has the potential to influence generations to come.

The Balance Between Aspiration and Integrity

While RDF empowers you to aim for the extraordinary, its true legacy lies in how it is wielded. A vision driven by integrity, empathy, and purpose creates genuine impact.

Key Principles for a Lasting Legacy

- **Stay Grounded:** Let your ambitions soar, but keep your values rooted.
- **Lead with Empathy:** Understand the needs and

aspirations of others as you shape the future.
- **Be Transparent:** Authenticity builds trust, and trust sustains movements.

Quote for Reflection:

> *"Success is not how high you have climbed, but how you make a positive difference to the world."* —Roy T. Bennett

From Possibility to Reality

The ultimate power of RDF isn't just imagining the impossible—it's bringing it to life. By applying the strategies and mindset outlined in this book, you have the potential to close the gap between vision and execution, turning dreams into tangible, transformative outcomes.

A Final Challenge

As you close this chapter, ask yourself:

- What reality do you want to shape?
- Who will benefit from the future you create?
- How will you measure your legacy—not just in achievements, but in the lives you've touched?

Take bold steps forward. Trust in your vision, embrace the challenges, and let the power of the Reality Distortion Field guide you toward an extraordinary legacy.

The world is waiting for you to redefine what's possible. Will you answer the call?

Thank you for embarking on this journey. The tools are in your hands, and the future is yours to create. Go forth and shape your reality.

7

Appendix

Key Concepts and Definitions

To ensure a comprehensive understanding of the Reality Distortion Field (RDF), here's a quick reference guide for some key terms and concepts covered in the book:

1. **Reality Distortion Field (RDF):** A psychological environment or mindset in which the usual boundaries of what's considered possible are bent or altered, often leading to extraordinary achievements.
2. **Perception Management:** The act of influencing how people perceive reality to inspire, motivate, and achieve results that might initially seem unattainable.

3. **Cognitive Dissonance:** The mental discomfort that occurs when a person is confronted with information or ideas that conflict with their current beliefs or worldview.
4. **Visionary Leadership:** A leadership style that involves inspiring others with a compelling vision, challenging existing limitations, and motivating others to reach their full potential.
5. **Shared Vision:** A common goal or objective that aligns and inspires a group of people to work collaboratively toward achieving it.
6. **Possibility-Driven Culture:** An environment where people are encouraged to think outside the box, take risks, and embrace creativity without fear of failure.

Recommended Readings and Resources

To deepen your understanding of RDF and related philosophies, here are a few books, podcasts, and articles that will expand your knowledge on mindset, leadership, and the art of shaping reality:

Books:

- *"The Innovator's Dilemma"* by Clayton Christensen – A deep dive into disruptive innovation, perfect for understanding how new realities can be shaped within industries.

- *"Steve Jobs"* by Walter Isaacson: This biography provides an in-depth look at Jobs's life and includes discussions about his RDF, describing how he could persuade others to believe in ambitious visions and goals. Isaacson illustrates how this ability affected the teams working on projects like the Macintosh
- *"The Innovators: How a Group of Hackers, Geniuses, and Geeks Created the Digital Revolution"* by Walter Isaacson: While not exclusively focused on Jobs, this book discusses various innovators, including Jobs, and touches on the RDF as part of the narrative surrounding creativity and leadership in technology
- *"Start with Why"* by Simon Sinek – Understanding the power of purpose-driven leadership, which is central to RDF.
- *"The Art of Possibility"* by Rosamund Stone Zander and Benjamin Zander – An exploration of how shifting perception can unlock extraordinary possibilities.
- *"The Power of Now"* by Eckhart Tolle – While not directly related to RDF, this book explores the power of present-moment awareness, which complements the idea of challenging limiting beliefs.

Podcasts:

- *The Tim Ferriss Show* – Conversations with world-class performers who often discuss shifting perspectives and pushing the boundaries of reality.
- *How I Built This* by NPR – Stories of entrepreneurs and innovators who reshaped their industries and took risks that defied the status quo.
- *The Tony Robbins Podcast* – Insights from one of the world's most renowned motivational speakers, with a focus on achieving personal transformation.

Articles and Blogs:

- *Harvard Business Review* (www.hbr.org) – Articles on leadership, innovation, and transforming organizational culture.
- *Medium* – Check out writers like Ben Hardy and Shane Parrish, who explore the intersection of psychology, performance, and personal growth.

Exercises for Reinforcing RDF

The following exercises are designed to help you practice and reinforce the principles of the Reality Distortion Field in your own life.

Perception Shift Exercise

- Identify a situation in your life where you feel limited by circumstances (e.g., career, health, relationships).
- Now, write down three alternative perspectives on this situation. How could you see this challenge differently? What new opportunities might be hidden within the limitation?
- Spend 10 minutes visualizing how you would approach this situation if you fully believed it was possible to achieve success in it.

Visualization of the Future

- Set aside 15 minutes to vividly imagine your ideal future, one where everything has gone according to your vision.
- Don't just focus on the tangible goals but also on how you feel in this future reality. Write about it in as much detail as possible.

Affirmation and Reaffirmation Routine

- Create a set of empowering affirmations that align with your vision. These should be present-tense, action-oriented statements that reinforce your ability to shape your reality.
- Repeat them out loud every morning for 30 days. Track any shifts in your mindset or behavior.

RDF Networking Practice

- Reach out to someone in your professional or personal life who embodies a "reality-distorting" mindset.
- Spend time with them discussing how they approach challenges, how they think about possibilities, and what beliefs they hold that allow them to shape their reality. Write down your insights.

FAQ (Frequently Asked Questions)

Here are some common questions people ask when beginning to work with the Reality Distortion Field:

1. **Can RDF be harmful if used in the wrong way?**
   Yes. RDF can lead to overconfidence or unrealistic expectations if not managed with integrity. It's important to balance ambition with grounded awareness, ensuring that your actions align with ethical principles and positive impact.

2. **How do I know if I'm being authentic while using RDF?**
   Authenticity comes from being true to your values and your deeper purpose. RDF works

best when it's aligned with a meaningful vision and not driven solely by ego or personal gain.

3. **Can RDF help me overcome setbacks or failures?**
Absolutely. RDF allows you to reframe challenges as learning opportunities, helping you stay resilient and persistent in the face of adversity.

4. **How long does it take to master RDF?**
Mastery of RDF is a lifelong journey. The more you practice and apply it in different areas of your life, the more natural it becomes. Consistency is key.

www.ingramcontent.com/pod-product-compliance
Lightning Source LLC
Chambersburg PA
CBHW070942220526
45469CB00007B/2480